THE GIFT AFTER SALVATION

by
Billy B. Smith

Billy B. Smith Ministries Publications
P.O. Box 6078
Ft. Worth, Texas 76115 U.S.A.

ISBN 1-879612-01-1

ACKNOWLEDGMENTS

It is impossible to write a book like this one without the help and encouragement of those around you. To all of those who have helped and encouraged me to complete this book, I would like to say thank you.

I would like to give special thanks to:

My wife, Mary, and our children, Billy Wayne and Amy, for their patience and understanding during these long months of writing.

My pastor, Harold Nichols, who has been an encouragement to this ministry from its beginning.

Dr. Jerry Savelle, whose simple, down-to-earth teaching has been an encouragement and inspiration to write this book.

Vicki Mobberley, for helping me keep my Texas English from taking over and for all of the grammar corrections that were made. I could not have finished this book without you.

Bill Nelon and David Gieger, for your part in helping me edit this book.

CONTENTS

INTRODUCTION

I was not raised in a Christian home, but I had touches of God throughout my life. My grandmother would sometimes take me to a little Baptist church; other times she would send me to either the Nazarene church or the Church of Christ with our neighbors. None of this was on a regular basis, and as the years passed, it was less and less until I did not go at all.

When I reached the age of 21, I found myself without God, miserable in life, trying to be someone I wasn't. I was always afraid of what others would think. This drove me to drinking whiskey, so that at the age of 21, I was drinking one quart of whiskey every day.

By the age of 22, I also found myself a physical wreck. My body had gone through many operations and sicknesses. Both feet and both knees had been operated on. I had suffered three heart attacks by the time I was 21 years old: my first at the age of 12, my second at the age of 19, and my third at the age of 21. I was also a diabetic. At this time I was having three to four epileptic seizures per day. I had to have two back surgeries and also two hernia surgeries. On top of all of this, I found that my home was falling apart.

It was at this time that God sent an old friend into my life to tell me about a God who would change my life, my situations, and even heal my body. This seemed just too unreal, but I had no other hope. So I went to church **just to listen**, and also to get him off my back about visiting his church.

That morning, as I began to listen to the visiting evangelist tell about the love of God and the price His Son had paid for me, my heart began to cry out to God. This is what I was looking for. I found that God was not trying to send me to hell nor trying to punish me for all my mistakes. He wasn't even putting sickness and disease on me to punish me. **He just wanted to love me.**

That day I gave up my old life of misery and started walking in a new life where the guilt of the past was gone and I didn't have to try to be someone else. I could just be me. I could not explain why, but I felt so free. I was free like a bird, and there was so much love coming out of my heart where there had been so much hate. God had given me a **new heart.**

I began to see many changes that were now taking place in my life simply because I had accepted Jesus as my Savior. I found myself wanting to find out all I could about God and His Son, Jesus.

The more I found out about Jesus, the more I wanted to be like Him. I wanted His peace, His joy, His boldness, His confidence, and His strength. There had to be some kind of secret to having all of this, and I believed it must be in this book called the Bible. This book was written about Jesus, and if I studied it, I could be like Him. I had lived a life of feeling like a failure, and I did not want to follow a failure. I wanted to follow a winner.

John 15:7-11

"If you abide in Me, and My words abide in you, ask whatever you wish, and it shall be done for you. By this is My Father glorified, that you bear much fruit, and so prove to be My disciples. Just as the Father has loved Me, I have also loved you; abide in My love. If you keep My commandments, you will abide in My love; just as I have kept My Father's commandments, and abide in His love. These things I have spoken to you, that My joy be in you, and that your joy may be made full."

As I began to put His words inside of me, I found that **John 14:12-17 and 23-26** were becoming a reality in my life.

"Truly, truly, I say to you, he who believes in Me, the works that I do shall he do also; and greater works than these shall he do; because I go to the Father. And whatever you ask in My name, that will I do, that the Father may be glorified in the Son. If you ask Me anything in My name, I will do it. If you love Me, you will keep My commandments. And I will ask the Father, and He will give you another Helper, that He may be with you forever; that is the Spirit of truth, whom the world cannot receive, because it does not behold Him or know

*Him, but you know Him because He abides
with you, and will be in you.*

*"If anyone loves Me, he will keep My word;
and My Father will love him, and We will
come to him, and make Our abode with him.
He who does not love Me does not keep My
words; and the word which you hear is not
Mine, but the Father's who sent Me. These
things I have spoken to you, while abiding
with you. But the **Helper, the Holy Spirit,**
whom the Father will send in My name, He
will teach you all things, and bring to your
remembrance all that I said to you."*

In this book, I will be sharing with you how I
learned to walk in the power and authority of God's
Word and how to use the weapons of our warfare
provided to us through His Word and the Holy
Spirit.

1

WHY DO PEOPLE
NOT SERVE GOD?

I have been a Christian for over twenty years now. My reasons for not serving God the first half of my life were no different than all the excuses I hear today. I can only find one true reason that people do not become Christians.

Hosea 4:6
My people are destroyed for lack of knowledge.

If we don't know the truth about God, we will not want to serve Him. If we think He wants us to be punished and go to hell, then we do not go to Him for forgiveness of sin. If we think God is putting sickness and disease on us to teach us something, then we do not go to Him for healing.

In order for us to have a lack of knowledge about anything, then somewhere there must be that knowledge. We have just not found it and appropriated it. I find in most cases that we have believed a lie about God because we did not know the truth about Him.

John 10:10

> *"The thief* [Satan] *comes only to steal, and kill, and destroy; I* [Jesus] *came that they might have life, and might have it abundantly."*

Satan told us lies to keep us from becoming Christians, and if we saw past those lies and became Christians anyway, then he told us lies to keep us from claiming the promises of God for ourselves. I find that most people believe some of these lies.

John 8:32

> Jesus said, *"You shall know the truth and the truth shall make you free."*

Where Do We Find the Truth?

Psalm 119:160

> *Thy word is truth.*

John 1:1

> *In the beginning was the Word, and the Word was with God, and the Word was God.*

Psalm 107:20

> *He sent His word and healed them, and delivered them from their destructions.*

God and His Word are the same. He sent His Word to us that we might know about Him and that we might know Him and His will for us. We cannot afford to believe everything people tell us that God's Word says. We can only believe the things we check out for ourselves in God's Word. I tell people not to believe me just because I say something, but to believe me because you can confirm what I say in God's Word. I could make a mistake or someone could have told me a lie that I believed.

Forgiveness of Sin—Is It For All?

From the time of the fall of man in the Garden of Eden, God has made a way for man to have fellowship with Him. Sin cannot come into the presence of God, so God covered the sin until a better way could be brought into being.

In Genesis 3:21, we can see where the first shedding of blood took place as a covering for sin, so that man could still come into God's presence.

In **Isaiah 53:3-6**, we find God's promise of the soon-coming Savior.

He was despised and forsaken of men, a man of sorrows, and acquainted with grief; and like one from whom men hide their face, He was despised, and we did not esteem Him.
Surely our griefs He Himself bore, and our sorrows He carried; yet we ourselves esteemed Him stricken, smitten of God, and afflicted.

> *But He was pierced through for our trans-*
> *gressions, He was crushed for our iniqui-*
> *ties; the chastening for our well-being fell*
> *upon Him, and by His scourging we are*
> *healed.*
> *All of us like sheep have gone astray, each*
> *of us has turned to his own way; but the*
> *Lord has caused the iniquity of us all to fall*
> *on Him.*

This Savior would no longer cover sin, but He would wipe it away forever.

Romans 3:24-25 (KJV)
> *Being justified freely by His grace through*
> *the redemption that is in Christ Jesus:*
> *Whom God hath set forth to be a propitia-*
> *tion through faith in his blood, to declare*
> *his righteousness for the remission of sins*
> *that are past, through the forbearance of*
> *God.*

God **remits** our sins and never remembers them again.

Psalm 103:12
> *As far as the east is from the west, so far*
> *has He removed our transgressions from us.*

We need to understand that all of these scriptures are talking about Jesus, and because of this, I want to tell you what God's Word says about Him.

John 3:16

"For God so loved the world, that He gave His only begotten Son, that whoever believes in Him should not perish, but have eternal life." That is talking about you and me.

1 John 4:14

We have beheld and bear witness that the Father has sent the Son to be the Savior of the world."

The Samaritans had this to say about Jesus:

John 4:40-42

So when the Samaritans came to Him they were asking Him to stay with them; and He stayed there two days. And many more believed because of His word; and they were saying to the woman, "It is no longer because of what you said that we believe, for we have heard for ourselves and know that this One is indeed the Savior of the world."

Jesus is not **waiting** on us to find Him.

Luke 19:10

*"For the Son of Man has **come to seek and save** that which was lost."*

Many people feel like God wants to save only certain people. That's not true.

Acts 10:34-35

*"God is not one to show **partiality,** but in every nation the man who fears Him and does what is right, is welcome to Him."*

Salvation is a gift of God; it is not something we can earn or buy.

Ephesians 2:8-9

*For by grace you have been saved through faith; and that not of yourselves, it is the **gift of God;** not as a result of works, that no one should boast.*

God has made the gift of salvation so easy to obtain that some people refuse to accept it because of their pride. But if we will simply believe in God's Word and confess it with our mouths, we will receive God's provision.

Romans 3:21-23

*But now apart from the Law the righteousness of God has been manifested, being witnessed by the Law and the Prophets, even the righteousness of God through **faith** in Jesus Christ for all those who believe; for there is no distinction; for all have sinned and fall short of the glory of God.*

16

Romans 6:23

*For the wages of sin is death, but the **free gift of God** is eternal life in Christ Jesus our Lord.*

As we read and hear God's Word, we can see that it is God's will for us to be forgiven of our sins, and faith will then begin to build inside of us so that we might reach out and take the gift God is offering to us.

Romans 10:17

So faith comes from hearing, and hearing by the word of Christ.

Romans 10:8-13

*"THE WORD IS NEAR YOU, IN YOUR MOUTH AND IN YOUR HEART"—that is, the word of faith which we are preaching, that if **you confess** with your mouth Jesus as Lord, and believe in your heart that God raised Him from the dead, you shall be saved; for with the heart man believes, resulting in righteousness, and with the mouth he confesses, resulting in salvation. For the Scripture says, "WHOEVER BELIEVES IN HIM WILL NOT BE DISAPPOINTED." For there is no distinction between Jew and Greek; for the same Lord is Lord of all, abounding in riches for all who call upon Him; for "WHOEVER WILL CALL UPON*

*THE NAME OF THE LORD WILL BE
SAVED."*

It takes action on our part to reach out and take
the gift God has provided for us through faith in His
Word. When we do this, something happens. Our
sins are forgiven, never remembered again, and we
become new people.

2 Corinthians 5:17-18
*Therefore if any man is in Christ, he is a
new creature; the old things passed away;
behold, new things have come. Now all
these things are from God, who reconciled
us to Himself through Christ.*

When we believe and confess Jesus as our
Savior, we are born again, and we are forgiven as if
we never did anything wrong. The problem here is
that even though God has forgiven us and placed
our sins in the sea of forgetfulness, never to be
remembered again by Him, we allow the devil to
bring this past up to us, and we cannot forgive ourselves. We must forgive ourselves and allow God to
help us put our past in the sea of forgetfulness. The
Bible says we are babes in Christ. Because Jesus
has gone to be with the Father in heaven, it would
seem almost impossible for babies to survive in this
world alone. But Jesus has not left us alone.

2

THE GIFT
AFTER SALVATION

Hebrews 13:5-6
> *"I WILL NEVER DESERT YOU, NOR WILL I EVER FORSAKE YOU," so that we confidently say, "THE LORD IS MY **HELPER**, I WILL NOT BE AFRAID."*

Jesus tells us that He must go to the Father, but that He will not leave us alone. He was always thinking about our needs. Listen to what He has to say to you and me.

John 16:7,13
> *"But I tell you the truth, it is to your advantage that I go away; for if I do not go away, the **Helper** shall not come to you; but if I go, I will send Him to you.*
> *"But when He, the **Spirit of truth,** comes, He will guide you into all the truth; for He will not speak on His own initiative, but*

whatever He hears, He will speak; and He will disclose to you what is to come."

Jesus has not left us alone—far from it. He has sent the Holy Spirit to be with us on His behalf. The Holy Spirit will never let us down. The Holy Spirit will do everything Jesus would do for us because He is acting on behalf of Jesus.

I really like how The Amplified Bible describes the work of the Holy Spirit.

John 14:15-17 (AMP)
*If you [really] love Me, you will keep (obey) My commands. And I will ask the Father, and He will give you another **Comforter (Counselor, Helper, Intercessor, Advocate, Strengthener, and Standby)**, that He may remain with you forever—The **Spirit of Truth,** Whom the world cannot receive (welcome, take to its heart), because it does not see Him or know and recognize Him. But you know and recognize Him, for He lives with you [constantly] and will be in you.*

The Holy Spirit Has a Three-fold Job in the World Today

1. The Holy Spirit **convicts** the world of sin. Without the convicting power of the Holy Spirit there would be no Church.

2. The Holy Spirit's second job is to **build up** and **edify** and **strengthen** the individual believer.
3. The Holy Spirit's third job is to **build up** and **edify** and **strengthen** the body of Christ (the Church).

John 16:8 (AMP)

*And when He comes, He will **convict and convince** the world and bring demonstration to it about sin and about righteousness (uprightness of heart and right standing with God) and about judgment.*

Jesus thought the Holy Spirit was so important to believers that He commanded the disciples to wait until they had received this gift before they departed to do the work of the ministry.

Acts 1:2-5

*Until the day when He was taken up, after He had **by the Holy Spirit** given orders to the apostles whom He had chosen. To these He also presented Himself alive, after His suffering, by many **convincing proofs,** appearing to them over a period of forty days, and speaking of the things concerning the kingdom of God.*
*And gathering them together, He **commanded** them not to leave Jerusalem, but to wait for what the Father had promised, "Which," He said, "you heard of from Me;*

*for John baptized with water, but you shall be baptized with the **Holy Spirit** not many days from now."* (This is also found in Matthew 3:11.)

Even though these men and women were believers, they were no different than Jesus. They needed the power of the Holy Spirit in their lives. The Holy Spirit anointed Jesus with power and authority to preach the gospel and to do all of the miracles He did. It is this same gift that Jesus wants you and me to have.

Matthew 12:18
"BEHOLD, MY SERVANT WHOM I HAVE CHOSEN; MY BELOVED IN WHOM MY SOUL IS WELL-PLEASED; I WILL PUT MY SPIRIT UPON HIM, AND HE SHALL PROCLAIM JUSTICE TO THE GEN-TILES."

Luke 4:18
"THE SPIRIT OF THE LORD IS UPON ME, BECAUSE HE ANOINTED ME TO PREACH THE GOSPEL TO THE POOR. HE HAS SENT ME TO PROCLAIM RELEASE TO THE CAPTIVES, AND RECOVERY OF SIGHT TO THE BLIND, TO SET FREE THOSE WHO ARE DOWN-TRODDEN, TO PROCLAIM THE FAVOR-ABLE YEAR OF THE LORD."

Acts 10:38

"You know of Jesus of Nazareth, how God anointed Him with the HOLY SPIRIT and with power, and how He went about doing good, and healing all who were oppressed by the devil; for God was with Him."

There is no record of Jesus ever performing any kind of miracle, or healing anyone, until the day the Holy Spirit came on Him. You don't read about Him having any major confrontations with the devil until He received the Holy Spirit. It was from the point when Jesus received the gift of the Holy Spirit that He began to do the mighty works of God.

The Bible tells us that Jesus did enough miracles to fill up all the books ever written (see John 21:25) if they were all recorded. This was all done in a period of three years after He received the Holy Spirit.

If Jesus needed the Holy Spirit and thought the disciples needed the Holy Spirit, what makes us think we don't need the Holy Spirit also?

For years we have listened to the lies of the devil, when he said this infilling of the Holy Spirit passed away with the apostles. It was so hard for me to believe this lie because as I read the Bible, I kept coming up with people who were not there on the Day of Pentecost who were still receiving the infilling of the Holy Spirit, and they had the same experiences that the apostles had. I could not get away from **Hebrews 13:8:**

Jesus Christ is the same yesterday and today, yes and forever.

Some people teach that the Holy Spirit and His power were only for the Early Church to establish itself, but nothing could be further from the truth. I would like to establish a few facts about the Holy Spirit.

Who is the Holy Spirit?

The Holy Spirit is the third member of the Godhead spoken of in Matthew 28:19, where Jesus told the apostles to go into all nations making disciples and *"baptizing them in the name of the Father and the Son and the Holy Spirit."*

The Holy Spirit, who is called **the Spirit of Truth, our Comforter, our Counselor, our Helper, our Advocate, our Intercessor, our Strengthener, our Standby, our Teacher,** has been given to us (the Church) to take the place of Jesus, to represent Jesus, and to act on His behalf to bring to our remembrance all things that Jesus has said to us and help us become Christlike (see John 14:26; 15:26; 16:7-8, 13-14; also Jude 20, Amplified).

Jesus and the Holy Spirit have been with the Father from the very beginning of time until now, helping in the creation, bringing you and me back into right standing with the Father, and teaching us all things that the Father has said to us (see Genesis 1:1-2 and John 1:1).

Who is the Holy Spirit For?

Joel 2:28

> *"And it will come about after this that I will pour out My Spirit on all mankind; and your sons and daughters will prophesy, your old men will dream dreams, your young men will see visions."*

In this verse, Joel is telling us about the coming of the Holy Spirit and the gifts that would function through the Holy Spirit.

We have already read in Acts 1:4-5, where Jesus gathered the apostles together and commanded them to wait until they had received the Holy Spirit. What caught my attention was reading Acts 2:38-39. Then I knew it was true—the Holy Spirit was for me also. Besides, God's Word says He is no respecter of persons. If the Christians in the Book of Acts needed the Holy Spirit, then I needed Him also.

Acts 2:38-39

> *"Repent, and let each of you be baptized in the name of Jesus Christ for the forgiveness of your sins; and you shall receive the **gift of the Holy Spirit.** For this promise is for **you** and **your children,** and for **all** who are far off, as many as the Lord our God shall call unto Himself."*

As a missionary in 33 different countries, I am seeing the miracle of Pentecost being poured out on all denominations around the world. I know of no Christian denomination that is not experiencing the charismatic movement in some way.

As I said earlier, the reason most people do not accept the price Jesus paid for their sins is because they do not know what He really did for them. I also believe that people do not seek after the baptism of the Holy Spirit because they do not have the knowledge of what the Holy Spirit can and will do for them and through them.

The Holy Spirit in Your Vocation

There is another aspect of the work of the Holy Spirit that is very seldom talked about, and I want us to look at this part for a moment.

1 Samuel 10:6

*"Then the Spirit of the Lord will come upon you mightily, and you shall prophesy with them and be changed into **another man**."*

When the Spirit of the Lord comes upon people, something must happen. With God's Spirit on you, you cannot be normal. In the New Testament when God's Spirit came on the believers, they cast out devils, healed the sick, raised the dead, and stilled the storms. You can plainly see this is not normal for human beings.

Let us look and see what happens when we come into God's presence and obey His commandments, given to us by His Spirit.

Deuteronomy 28:1-14

"Now it shall be, if you will diligently obey the Lord your God, being careful to do all His commandments which I command you today, the Lord your God will set you high above all the nations of the earth. And all these blessings shall come upon you and overtake you, if you will obey the Lord your God.

"Blessed shall you be in the city, and blessed shall you be in the country. Blessed shall be the offspring of your body and the produce of your ground and the offspring of your beasts, the increase of your herd and the young of your flock. Blessed shall be your basket and your kneading bowl. Blessed shall you be when you come in, and blessed shall you be when you go out.

"The Lord will cause your enemies who rise up against you to be defeated before you; they shall come out against you one way and shall flee before you seven ways.

*"The Lord will command the blessing upon you in your barns and in all that **you put your hands to,** and He will bless you in the land which the Lord your God gives you.*

"The Lord will establish you as a holy people to Himself, as He swore to you, if you will keep the commandments of the Lord your God, and walk in His ways. So all the peoples of the earth shall see that you are

*called by the name of the Lord; and they
shall be afraid of you.*

*"And the Lord will make you abound in
prosperity, in the offspring of your body and
in the offspring of your beast and in the produce of your ground, in the land which the
Lord swore to your fathers to give you. The
Lord will open for you His good storehouse,
the heavens, to give rain to your land in its
season and to bless all the work of your
hand; and you shall lend to many nations,
but you shall not borrow.*

*"And the Lord shall make you the head and
not the tail, and you only shall be above,
and you shall not be underneath, if you will
listen to the commandments of the Lord
your God, which I charge you today, to
observe them carefully, and do not turn
aside from any of the words which I command you today, to the right or to the left, to
go after other gods to serve them."*

All through these promises of God, there is one
thing I kept noticing. There is a part we must play
in receiving these blessings. **We must hear. We
must obey. We must put our hands to the task.
God cannot bless what we do not do.**

We seem to have no problem seeing that God
wants to bless the Church with the gifts of the Spirit,
because these are for the Church. But now we are
talking about God anointing and blessing what we
do in our vocation and for our own families.

Will God really do this? Yes! He will. I believe I can show you that He not only will, but that He has, and that He is doing these things today.

Hebrews 13:8

Jesus Christ is the same yesterday and today, yes and forever.

Acts 10:34

"I most certainly understand now that God is not one to show partiality."

With this in mind, I want us to look in the Old Testament and see how God anointed men with His Spirit to do the labor of their hands. He gave them wisdom and knowledge and understanding to do this labor.

Exodus 28:3

"And you shall speak to all the skillful persons whom I have endowed with the spirit of wisdom, that they make Aaron's garments to consecrate him, that he may minister as priest to Me."

Exodus 31:3

"And I have filled him with the Spirit of God in wisdom, in understanding, in knowledge, and in all kinds of craftsmanship."

He also anointed men and women the same way in the New Testament.

In 1 Corinthians 12:28, Paul is telling us of the gifts of *helps* and *administrations*. I believe this is talking about the craftsmen among us; that is, those who use their crafts and abilities for the Church as well as in their vocations.

God wants to be involved in every part of our lives, and any part of our lives that we yield to Him, He will bless.

In these scriptures, God has revealed how it is He who gives us skills and abilities that we possess. It is He who gives us the power and ability to make wealth.

Deuteronomy 8:18

"But you shall remember the Lord your God, for it is He who is giving you power to make wealth."

When you look at what *power* means here, it means "wisdom, ability, strength to get wealth." It takes the anointing of God for you and me to walk in the blessings of God. There are many people who seem to have the natural ability to do anything but keep failing. Before I was born again I was walking in failure, and even after I was born again I was still a failure. This was because I had not met **the Counselor, the Helper, the Advocate, the Intercessor, the Strengthener, the Standby, or the Teacher.** I was like most people. I tried to do everything by myself and in my ability. You see, I had been to college; I did not need anyone else.

After I was filled with the Holy Spirit and began to pray in tongues on a regular basis, I began to notice impressions that I later discovered were directions of the Holy Spirit. I would be impressed to do a certain thing on my job and I would ignore the impression, thinking it was just me. Later I would find out that if I had obeyed the impression, I would not have erred.

The more I prayed in this language that the Holy Spirit gave me, the more these impressions would come to me on my job, about things concerning my job. I finally realized that these impressions were coming from God, and as I began to obey them, I found myself receiving pay increases and finally a promotion to a supervisory position.

It was at this time that God impressed me to change my profession completely. I said, "God, I have never done that type of work, and I don't know if I can do it." God gently spoke to me and said, "You can't, but I can. I will teach you how to do the job." I started on the job, and in just a few weeks I was doing better than most of the employees who had been there for years. Praise God! I also received a pay increase after only four weeks.

I have worked in six different professions, and the Holy Spirit helped me learn every one of them. Then God put me in places of leadership in those jobs.

As God once told me, "I want to help everyone—even the housewife and the janitor—but the problem is they never ask for My help. They try to do things in their own knowledge and ability and then they blame Me for their failures."

We must train ourselves to hear God's voice so we don't continue making the mistakes that have plagued us for so long. I will discuss more on the subject of hearing God's voice in a later book.

How Do We Receive This Gift of the Holy Spirit?

First I want us to understand that the Holy Spirit is a gift, and that as a gift, it is not forced on us. A gift is something we must **reach out and take possession of.**

Many people teach that we receive the Holy Spirit when we are born again, but that is not scriptural. There is a part that the Holy Spirit plays in our conversion to Christ. Remember, as we have said earlier, that the job of the Holy Spirit is to convict the world of sin and to convince the world of God's love for them with many infallible proofs. When the world has been convinced, then they will receive first the gift of salvation. Peter tells us that **we are born again by the Word of God**.

1 Peter 1:23 (KJV)
> *Being born again, not of corruptible seed, but of incorruptible, by the word of God, which liveth and abideth for ever.*

Romans 6:23

> For the wages of sin is death, but the **free gift** of God is eternal life in Christ Jesus our Lord.

To receive this gift, we must follow the instructions given to us in God's Word.

Romans 10:9-13

> That if you confess with your mouth Jesus as Lord, and believe in your heart that God raised Him from the dead, you shall be saved; for with the heart man believes, resulting in righteousness, and with the mouth he confesses, resulting in salvation. For the scripture says, "WHOEVER BELIEVES IN HIM WILL NOT BE DISAPPOINTED." For there is no distinction between Jew and Greek; for the same Lord is Lord of all, abounding in riches for all who **call** upon Him: for "WHOEVER WILL CALL UPON THE NAME OF THE LORD WILL BE SAVED."

The *new birth* is called "being born again," or "receiving eternal life." *The gift after salvation* is called **receiving the Holy· Spirit, the baptism of the Holy Spirit, or being filled with the Holy Spirit.**

Notice that in both salvation and in the baptism of the Holy Spirit, there is an act of receiving on our part. God does not force these gifts on us.

We must remember that when Jesus spoke to the disciples in Acts 1:1-5, He was speaking to believers. The Holy Spirit had already proven who Jesus was *by many convincing proofs* (Acts 1:3). Now Jesus tells them to wait until they have received this gift, the Holy Spirit, that He had promised them in John 14:26.

After the disciples had been filled with the Holy Spirit in Acts 2:4, the first thing Peter did was to tell us that this gift was not for the disciples only, but for all who call on the name of the Lord.

Acts 2:38-39

> *And Peter said to them, "Repent, and let each of you be baptized in the name of Jesus Christ for the forgiveness of your sins; and you shall receive the gift of the Holy Spirit. For this **promise** is for **you** and **your children**, and for **all** who are far off, as many as the Lord our God shall call to Himself."*

Now that we know this gift is for **all believers**, let us see how to receive this gift. First we must see that Jesus is the Baptizer in the Holy Spirit.

Matthew 3:11

> John the Baptist says, *"As for me, I baptize you with water for repentance, but He who is coming after me is mightier than I, and I am not fit to remove His sandals; **He will baptize you with the Holy Spirit and fire**."*

I would like for you to notice here that we have now received the gift of salvation from God the Father because of the gift of His Son Jesus to us. But also notice that we now have the right to receive the gift of the Holy Spirit because Jesus did not want to leave us alone, and He asked the Father to send this gift to us. Now we can see that Jesus is the one who baptizes us in the Holy Spirit.

I also want you to notice that just like the gift of salvation, the gift of the Holy Spirit is not forced on us. It is just offered to us, and we must ask for this gift.

Luke 11:13

"If you then, being evil, know how to give good gifts to your children, how much more shall your heavenly Father give the Holy Spirit to those who ask Him?"

I have many people say to me, "What if I ask for the Holy Spirit and I get something else?" Let us read.

Luke 11:9-13

"And I say to you, ask, and it shall be given to you; seek, and you shall find; knock, and it shall be opened to you. For everyone who asks, receives; and he who seeks, finds; and to him who knocks, it shall be opened.
"Now suppose one of you fathers is asked by his son for a fish; he will not give him a snake instead of a fish, will he? Or if he is

asked for an egg, he will not give him a scorpion, will he?

"If you then, being evil, know how to give good gifts to your children, how much more shall your heavenly Father give the Holy Spirit to those who ask Him?"

The answer to their question is: you will not get something else. If you ask for the Holy Ghost, that is exactly what is given to you. We must learn to simply take God at His word and quit letting the devil put the "what ifs" into our thinking.

Some people ask me, "Do I have to have the Holy Spirit?" **The answer is no.** You don't have to have the Holy Spirit; but if you want to be obedient to God, you must receive the Holy Spirit.

We have already seen in Acts 1:1-5 that Jesus commanded the disciples to receive the Holy Spirit. In Acts 2:38-39 we were shown that the Holy Spirit is for us also, not just for the disciples. But are we commanded to receive the Holy Spirit?

Ephesians 5:17-18

*So then do not be foolish, but **understand what the will of the Lord is.** And do not get drunk with wine, for that is dissipation, **but be filled with the Spirit.***

I believe it is very clear what the will of God is for you and me concerning receiving the Holy Spirit. I also believe it is very clear that we should ask to receive this gift of the Holy Spirit.

There Are Two Ways to Receive the Holy Spirit

Everything we receive from God comes by faith in His Word, whether it be salvation, or healing, or the gift of the Holy Spirit. We receive all of these gifts through trusting and obeying His Word.

First there is receiving the Holy Spirit by simply believing God's Word and accepting His gift as yours. When this happens, you just start functioning in this gift because you recognize that it is your gift. If it is yours, then you have the right to use it.

The second way is the most common way because most people need a point of contact. This is called the "laying on of hands." It is the same as in healing. Some receive by faith in God's Word, and others need a point of contact by either anointing with oil or laying on of hands. Either one of these will work in healing. In receiving the Holy Spirit, we just need to move where our faith is and receive this wonderful gift.

Peter emphasized the importance of believing God in receiving the Holy Spirit.

Acts 11:16-27 (KJV)

Then remembered I the word of the Lord, how that He said, John indeed baptized with water; but ye shall be baptized with the Holy Ghost. Forasmuch then as God gave them the like gift as He did unto us, who believed on the Lord Jesus Christ; what was I, that I could withstand God?

As Peter has just relayed to us, we can see that the disciples received the Holy Spirit by simply believing the Word of Jesus and that those at Cornelius's house received the Holy Spirit by simply believing the Word preached by Peter. Now we can see that this is one method of receiving the Holy Spirit.

Then there were those who received the Holy Spirit by the laying on of hands.

Acts 8:14-17

*Now when the apostles in Jerusalem heard that Samaria had received the word of God, they sent them Peter and John, who came down and prayed for them, that they might receive the Holy Spirit. For He had not yet fallen upon any of them; they had simply been baptized in the name of the Lord Jesus. **Then they began laying their hands on them and they were receiving the Holy Spirit.***

Acts 19:4-6

*Paul said, "John baptized with the baptism of repentance, telling the people to believe in Him who was coming after him, that is, in Jesus." And when they heard this, they were baptized in the name of the Lord Jesus. And when Paul had laid his hands upon them, the Holy Spirit came on them, and **they began speaking with tongues and prophesying.***

3

WHAT ABOUT TONGUES?

I often hear people say that they want to receive the Holy Spirit, but that they don't want those tongues. Well, I tell them, "I'm sorry, but they come together. You can't have one without the other."

Again I must say, the only reason anyone would not want the gift of the Holy Spirit with the evidence of speaking in tongues is because of a lack of knowledge of what the manifestation of tongues is and what it does for us.

To begin with, tongues is the initial evidence of the indwelling of the Holy Spirit. When we speak in tongues, we are yielding our tongues or allowing the Holy Spirit, the third member of the Godhead, to use our tongues to speak, to pray, and to sing through us. The Holy Spirit gives us the words to speak, but I must point out that we must do the speaking. We control what the Holy Spirit can or cannot do through our obedience to Him.

1. **The initial evidence of the Holy Spirit was tongues.**

Acts 2:4

*And they were all filled with the **Holy Spirit** and began to speak with other tongues, as the Spirit was giving them utterance.*

Acts 10:45-46

Jewish believers were amazed: *And all the circumcised believers who had come with Peter were amazed, because the gift of the Holy Spirit had been poured out upon the Gentiles also. **For they were hearing them speaking with tongues and exalting God.***

Acts 19:4-6

*Paul said, "John baptized with the baptism of repentance, telling the people to believe in Him who was coming after him, that is, in Jesus." And when they heard this, they were baptized in the name of the Lord Jesus. And when Paul had laid his hands upon them, the **Holy Spirit came on them, and they began speaking with tongues and prophesying.***

If God never changes and if people are still receiving the Holy Spirit today—**and they are**—then when they receive the Holy Spirit they should speak in tongues as they did in the Early Church. That is why in 1972 when I received the Holy Spirit, I expected to speak in tongues as they did at the beginning of the Church. If I had not spoken in tongues as Paul and others did, then I would have doubted my experience in the Holy Spirit.

2. Tongues is a sign to the non-believer.

1 Corinthians 14:22
So then tongues are for a sign, not to those who believe, but to unbelievers.

Mark 16:17 (AMP)
And these attesting signs will accompany those who believe: in My name they will drive out demons; they will speak in new languages.

Many times I hear people say, "I have brought a visitor to church today; I hope no one gives a message in tongues." They should hope that someone does give a message in tongues. I have never met anyone who was scared off when a message in tongues was spoken and the interpretation was given.

Many times they did not understand everything that was going on, but they recognized that it was a supernatural happening. This oftentimes draws people to the Lord because they know if God is God, then supernatural things take place.

I have been in services where a message was given and a non-believer was present. After the service he came up to the person who spoke in tongues and asked where he had learned the language he was speaking. It was the non-believer's language, and the one who had given the message did not know the language. Because of this supernatural experience, the person was born again. This type of experience has happened many times in our meetings. So you see, it is not to be feared; you should be excited about a message given in front of your visitor.

I believe the truth is that most of those who are fearing the supernatural act of the Holy Spirit are just afraid they cannot explain it to their friends. Don't try to explain; just tell them what God's Word says and be prepared to show them in the Scriptures. That is all you are responsible to do. It is the Holy Spirit's job to convince them, not yours.

3. Speaking in tongues edifies the believer.

1 Corinthians 14:4
One who speaks in a tongue edifies himself.

Jude 20
But you, beloved, building yourselves up on your most holy faith; praying in the Holy Spirit.

Romans 8:26-27
The Spirit also helps our weakness; for we do not know how to pray as we should, but the Spirit Himself intercedes for us with groanings too deep for words; and He who searches the hearts knows what the mind of

the Spirit is, because He intercedes for the
saints according to the will of God.

We must understand that when we are speaking in tongues, we are not speaking to men, but we are speaking directly to God. We must also realize there are many mysteries or divine secrets that we do not know or understand. But when we pray in tongues, then we are praying about those divine secrets or mysteries.

1 Corinthians 14:2-4 (Moffatt's translation):
"For he who speaks in a tongue addresses
God, not men; no one understands him; he
is talking of divine secrets in the Spirit. On
the other hand, he who prophesies address-
es men in words that edify, encourage, and
console them. He who speaks in a 'tongue'
edifies himself, whereas he who prophesies
edifies the church."

It is God's will for us to have the best of everything and to be healthy and prosper according to His Word in Deuteronomy 28. God created us and He loves us because He is our Heavenly Father, so when He prays, He prays for our best. According to 3 John 2, God is praying for our health and our prosperity. According to John 10:10, He is praying for us to have life abundantly—that means strength, joy, and peace in the Holy Spirit.

4. We can give thanks to God in tongues.

Not only can we pray for things we don't know how to pray for, but if we don't know how to thank God for all He has done or is doing, then we can also give thanks to God by praying in tongues.

1 Corinthians 14:15-17
I shall pray with the spirit and I shall pray with the mind also; I shall sing with the spirit and I shall sing with the mind also. **Otherwise if you bless the spirit only,** *how will the one who fills the place of the un-gifted say the "Amen" at your giving of thanks, since he does not know what you are saying?* **For you are giving thanks well enough,** *but the other man is not edified.*

How Can I Allow the Holy Spirit to Speak Through Me?

First we must recognize, as I have already said, that the Holy Spirit is a gift. Because it is a gift, God will not force anything on you. He will not force you to accept the Holy Spirit, and He will not force you to use the Holy Spirit by making you pray in tongues.

Romans 6:13 (KJV)
Paul says, *Yield yourselves unto God, as those that are alive from the dead,* **and your members as instruments of righteousness unto God.**

There is a lot of difference in you yielding yourself and your members to God, and God just taking possession. You must also realize that when you yield yourself to do something, you are still in control. It is the same with the Holy Spirit; we are in control of its use.

God is not a God of confusion.

1 Corinthians 14:27-33

*If anyone speaks in a tongue, it should be by two or at the most three, and each in turn, and let one interpret; but if there is no interpreter, let him keep silent in the church; and let him speak to himself and to God. And let two or three prophets speak, and let the others pass judgment. But if a revelation is made to another who is seated, let the first keep silent. For you can all prophesy one by one, so that all may learn and all may be exhorted; and the **spirits of prophets are subject to prophets; for God is not a God of confusion but of peace, as in all the churches of the saints.***

When I pray in tongues, I am doing the praying. I am yielding myself to the Spirit of God. I am doing the speaking with my tongue, but the Holy Spirit is giving me the utterance that I speak. Notice what Paul says.

1 Corinthians 14:15
> *I shall pray with the spirit and I shall pray with the mind also; I shall sing with the spirit and I shall sing with the mind also.*

Mark 16:17 (speaking about believers)
> *"They will speak with new tongues."*

You have a part in receiving the Holy Spirit with the evidence of speaking in tongues. Your part is to release your faith in God's Word that says if we ask the Father for the Holy Spirit, He will give it to us (see Luke 11:13). If we release faith, then that means we must act on our faith and speak out the sounds that the Holy Spirit gives to us.

James 2:17-18
> *Even so faith, if it has no works, is dead, being by itself. But someone may well say "You have faith, and I have works; show me your faith without the works, and I will show you my faith by my works."*

I have prayed for thousands of believers to receive the Holy Spirit with the evidence of speaking in tongues. I can say that I have never had anyone who would obey the instructions I am sharing with you, who did not have their prayer language manifested.

1. **Trust God not to give you a bad gift or one that will harm you.**

James 1:17

Every good thing bestowed and every per-fect gift is from above, coming down from the Father of lights, with whom there is no variation, or shifting shadow.

2. Ask according to Luke 11:13

"If you then, being evil, know how to give good gifts to your children, how much more shall your heavenly Father give the Holy Spirit to those who ask Him?"

Believe **John 14:14**

"If you ask Me anything in My name, I will do it."

3. Then, by an act of your faith, speak the first sound. Do not speak a known language or a sound known to you. If you will make the first sound, God will continue speaking because faith moves God.

Many people want to start speaking in their own language, thinking God will make them change languages. That will not happen. You can speak only one language at a time, so you speak either in tongues or in your natural language.

4. This is the point at which the sounds of your new prayer language will begin, but this is

also the point at which your mind and the devil will begin to fight you.

a. The first thought that comes is, "Where is this coming from? Am I making this up?"

b. At this point most people stop praying in this new language. **But don't stop.**

c. If other people are praying, they notice that they don't sound like everyone else, so they stop. **But don't stop.**

    I have prayed for 50 or 60 people at one time and none of them spoke the same language. God has many different languages.

d. By this time you should notice that these sounds are not coming from your head, because your mind is thinking all kinds of thoughts at the same time you are praying. Most people don't do well at thinking more than one thought at a time.

e. Next I encourage people to sing in tongues. Most of the time they try to tell me they don't know how to sing in the Spirit. I tell them that the words they speak in their natural language are the same words they use when they sing in their natural language. Now use the same words you are speaking in tongues with and let God put a tune with it.

f. I want people to be very sure of their experience with the Holy Spirit, so I have them stop and start praying in tongues several times. I do this until they feel comfortable praying in tongues.

g. Next I remind them that the Bible says the devil is a liar and the father of liars. I tell them this because he will tell them every lie he can think of to keep them from continuing in the development of their prayer life. He does not want them to be praying the will of God for their lives.

h. Last of all I remind them that Jude 20 says **if they pray in tongues,** they will be built up and edified. That also leaves us with the thought that **if you don't pray in tongues,** you will not be built up and edified.

Many people receive the Holy Spirit, but few are actually **filled with the Holy Spirit**. Many people receive the initial evidence of the infilling of the Holy Spirit, which is speaking in tongues, but never go any further in this experience with God. Jesus has given us the third member of the Godhead (the Holy Spirit) to fellowship with. The Holy Spirit is our **Teacher, Advocate, Standby, Strengthener, Helper**, and many other things, but He has also been given to us to give us **power to do the work of the ministry**.

Acts 1:8

"You shall receive power when the Holy Spirit has come upon you; and you shall be My witnesses both in Jerusalem, and in all Judea and Samaria, and even to the remotest part of the earth."

The word used for *power* here, in the Greek, is *dunamis. Dunamis* is the word from which we get the word *dynamite*. When we receive the Holy Spirit, we have abiding in us the explosive, supernatural, divine power that it took to create heaven and earth and everything that is in it. The Holy Spirit is often referred to as "a river of life" that flows out of us.

John 7:37-39

"If any man is thirsty, let him come to Me and drink. He who believes in Me, as the Scripture said, 'From his innermost being shall flow rivers of living water.' But this He spoke of the Spirit, whom those who believed in Him were to receive; for the Spirit was not yet given, because Jesus was not yet glorified."

The only thing that can stop a river from flowing is if someone or something dams it up. The only one who can stop the flow of the Holy Spirit is the one who possesses this gift; he or she has total control of this gift. Too many people receive the Holy Spirit with the evidence of speaking in tongues but do not continue with this life-giving flow from God (communication between you and God).

If you immerse a glass in a pan of water and leave it there, the water will become stagnant and the glass will become dirty, and no one will use it. If you are baptized in the Holy Spirit and do nothing with this experience, your experience will also stagnate.

When you are filled with the Holy Spirit, you are filled with a dynamite-like power, an explosive-like power that causes miracles and demonstrations to take place. This is to convince the world of Jesus and of His power. You are also filled with a boldness that will proclaim Jesus, no matter what the obstacles may be, even to the threatenings of death.

Acts 4:29-31

> *"And now, Lord, take note of their threats, and grant that Thy bond-servants may speak Thy word with all confidence, while Thou dost extend Thy hand to heal, and signs and wonders take place through the name of Thy holy servant Jesus."*

Ephesians 5:18 (AMP)

Do not get drunk with wine, for that is debauchery; but ever be filled and stimulated with the [Holy] Spirit.

In the original Greek, that scripture means to be continually being filled with the Holy Spirit.

In Acts 4:29-33, the disciples are being refilled with the Holy Spirit, and in Ephesians 5:18, we are told to continue being filled with the Holy Spirit.

From my own personal experiences, I have found that as I minister and give out of that river of life that flows out of me, I grow weak after several hours of ministry. I begin praying in the Holy Spirit, and shortly I find that I am strong again and ready to give out once more. It is important to us and to those who we will minister to that we be built up and edified by praying in the Holy Spirit.

Jude 20

But you, beloved, building up yourselves on your most holy faith; praying in the Holy Spirit.

Notice, you build yourself up by praying in the Holy Spirit. So that would leave us with the thought that if we don't pray in the Holy Spirit, we won't be built up. When God gives you a gift, He expects you to use that gift. If you don't, it is not God's fault.

Have You Accepted Christ?

If you have read this book and you are not sure that you have been born again, or if you have never **personally** asked Jesus to come into your life and forgive you of your sins, I invite you to pray the following prayer with me. According to Romans 10:9-13, you must personally ask God to forgive you of your sins. No one can do this for you.

Romans 10:9-13

If you confess with your mouth Jesus as Lord, and believe in your heart that God raised Him from the dead, you shall be saved; for with the heart man believes, resulting in righteousness, and with the mouth he confesses, resulting in salvation. For the Scripture says, "WHOEVER BELIEVES IN HIM WILL NOT BE DISAPPOINTED." For there is no distinction between Jew and Greek; for the same Lord is Lord of all, abounding in riches for all who call upon Him; for "WHOEVER WILL CALL UPON THE NAME OF THE LORD WILL BE SAVED."

If you believe that Jesus died to pay the price for your sins and that God raised Him from the dead, **repeat this prayer with me:**

God, I am a sinner. Please forgive me of my sins. I accept Your Son, Jesus, as my

Savior, and I accept the price He paid for my sins (His blood).

Now, Father, I promise that I will read Your Word so I can find out what a Christian is like, and then I will act like a Christian. I will go to church on a regular basis—not just once or twice a year—so I can grow strong through the strength and encouragement of fellow Christians. I realize that we need each other. When I am weak, my church family will help and encourage me, and when others are weak, I will help and encourage them.

Father, because You have just forgiven me, I now forgive myself. I don't have the right to hold on to the things You have forgiven. Your Word says that my sins will never be remembered again. I thank You for this.

Father, I forgive those who have hurt me, and I ask that You also forgive them. I know they were deceived by Satan just as I was. Please send someone to tell them about Jesus so they too can become Christians. Thank You, Father. Amen.